Life on the Edge

poems by

Nancy Wheaton

Finishing Line Press
Georgetown, Kentucky

Life on the Edge

ACKNOWLEDGMENTS

ALL poems, EXCEPT "Haunted House", "Olive Moon" and "Life on the
Edge" have been previously published.

I would like to acknowledge and thank:
Brian Evans-Jones, as a poet and mentor
Carol Bachofner, as a poet and mentor and friend

I would also like to thank my children:
Patrick, Daniel, Oneta and Katharine

Publisher: Leah Huete de Maines
Editor: Christen Kincaid
Cover Art: Breehan James, *August Sunset*
Author Photo: Sherry Madden
Cover Design: Elizabeth Maines McCleavy

Order online: www.finishinglinepress.com
also available on amazon.com

Author inquiries and mail orders:
Finishing Line Press
PO Box 1626
Georgetown, Kentucky 40324
USA

Contents

Spanish Sparrows

The language seems the same; brown and tan birds twirl
and sing from the rooftop, while another trio
searches for food scraps. A different pair blends
into the bark, watches, heads jerk to the right,
back to the middle, then left. They flit near the beehive.

Earlier this summer, I watched a male sparrow
from my New Hampshire porch. He repeated his monotonous
song as he watched his female: procumbent, dead
in the middle of the yard. He sang for a week. Alone.
Other females visited. He harangued them away.

Here in Zaragoza, the sparrows and I,
on this hot, dry and windless afternoon,
share the siesta. I am the same capering,
exhausted woman. Is it a *marvelous error*, as Machado
writes, to believe that *the bees make honey from my old failures?*

Goldilocks Zone

Planets or moons located in the Goldilocks zone are at the right distance from their star so that they're not too hot and not too cold—just like Baby Bear's porridge in the fairy tale. Their overall temperature is just right for the formation of liquid. Water, a landmark of life.particle.scitech.org.au

Today I learn of two deaths;
Both battling illnesses before surrender.
I remember Arthur
who ran with me,
mentored me into a safe zone,
away from despair. Into
constantly flowing questions.

And the reverend Dr. Hilson who believed
in God's ever present love. I recall
he comforted the mother of an addicted
student. What do we know
of the Will of God? Me?
I want my friends back.
I want do-overs.

Last year I met a man on the Toronto tram,
homeless. I tried to identify the smell.
Urine? Unwashed clothing? I made
a face to my standing friend. Our stop
was half a mile away. And I knew shame.
My mildewed conscience
and smelly self shrunk as I sat next
to him. Reached over for his hand.

The Hubble telescope remains pointed
at fixed spaces. After a while, when
the stars give up the spotlight, shapes
emerge. This planetary just right place,
in the shadows, is this the waiting
room of another Realm? I am caught! We descend
and rain from a sudden downpour trickles
into the half-open buttonholes of my shirt.

Sailing from Le Havre

We board the S. S. America up the ramp me holding
my four year old sister's hand Dad smoking Mom in sunglasses
wrapping the dog leash tighter up and up we walk A young steward
shows us the cabin tells us to *be on deck* for safety instructions
with all the others In the June weather breeze I overhear a woman

crying she doesn't want to go to Boston after Kennedy's assassination
how everything will be too hard to manage and my older brother
carrying our two year old sister My dad grips his wrist I can feel the hard
    squeeze
Dad reminds him to be in charge of his sisters oh I smell the vodka see
the cigarette and the smile and tip to the steward I am focused, serious
and hear his whisper *stop pouting* my sister is smiling and waving at the
    waves
tugging me over to the side We see the churning green and ivory
inhale the sea and I know why she is happy Suddenly I am warned
by the steward to stay away from the railing and I feel another hard flick
on my arm We put on life vests as the sea rolls, as my head churns
with the sea I understand that later after more vodka the younger sisters
asleep the deck chair conversations with other officers and wives over
    aperitifs
more cigarettes we will slide under the ropes blocking stairways We will
    climb
to the top layer of the ship gasp at shooting stars imitate our father's
clenched and clipped words find comfort laughing while the sea trundles
    on

When Stones Fly

A gush of snow
rushing down the Ohio river
and the hurricane blowing
up the coast of Florida both push
stones to new places—
into wet grooves,
clear water over moss-covered
rocks with faded and topless acorns
that lie stuck in the crevices, just like
you feel when you walk the river
shore near the new neighborhood.
Here, women wear false eyelashes
and walk their pugs in cable-knits sweaters.

You are from another stone scenario.
In your old neighborhood, bags of shore rocks
were picked up and moved away from the sea,
from their familiar sand and seaweed safety.
The stones are meant to repair an historic fence.
You walk by two brothers who lay granite
tiles in a driveway. They bicker over placement;
one standing in the street for perspective,
the other lifting and fitting the tiles into the mosaic
of grays. The stones settle—
as if this manufactured growth will wash
away the memory of annihilation.

Below the Surface

The marsh empties

        into a pond
where geese lounge

    in the afternoon,

where mice scamper

       amid the reeds,
  where walkers

    like me, pause

         to block out car noise
    I want to slip

into this water scene

           with tall grasses,
  and ripples on the surface

I can feel those

        sudden water spider blips

atop this green, craggy fluid,

       unfamiliar comforting

this place where I hear a

     whisper   *here — come here*

Watch for Falling Ice

When the snow blows—
big flakes that dip and alight,
and early chickadees dive among
the white delicate shapes—well, it all
seems so idyllic until the sleet
begins. A sudden shift into a penetrating cold
like Boris and Natasha in *Rockie and Bullwinkle*
who sneer: *everyone has a job to do.*
The chickadees dart to the maples.
I shovel mounting flakes. Slip.
And again. Black Ice. Just as slinky
as Natasha's form-fitting dress.

Haunted House

Owned by an elderly couple,
the modern A-frame of dark
wood and large triangular
windows stood facing the river.

Stephanie and I ran
through nearby woods, told
secrets and talked about boys.
Picked wildflowers. Waved to the couple.

I noticed it first. The grass
no longer mown, the weeds
creeping around the driveway.
The temperature dropped at their driveway.

Turns out the couple went
together to the only Nursing Home in town.
Childless. Every real estate
agent wanted the listing.

They said NO to selling. This was prime
property, yet I heard no one;
not their minister nor their grocery
man could convince them.

The windows clouded. The city
sent a man to mow the lawn
but the gardens remained untended.
Only the tiger lilies bloomed.

Late that fall, Stephanie was diagnosed.
Leukemia. Youth favored her, still she
would take Tasigna for the rest
of her days. Live with a limp.

I floated in the river one very hot day.
Closed my eyes to the frigid ongoing fighting
at home. Oh! I landed in front of the house!
Smaller somehow. A timbered succor.

An Afternoon Vivaldi Concerto

She sits in a green velour chair,
waving at strangers rushing
past her in a carpeted hall.

In this elegant home
without an odor of urine or loneliness,
she sits in a green velour chair.

A Vivaldi concerto from her CD collection
softly plays at the nurse's station while
her eyes wander again to the hall.

Her fingers lift, stretch. Ready to begin.
She remembers. Facing the door, she gazes
outward. She sits in a green velour chair.

An orderly delivers a bouquet of yellow roses,
a gift from her only son who gets up
then sits down again, still waiting in the hall,

unable to enter. Adrift, tired, his marriage
ending. She sits in a green velour chair.
He stands in the hall.

The Green Flash

Each second the earth is struck hard by 4.5 pounds of sunlight.
We are hi-jacked by a vision of an ivory sprawl. On our very planet
an entry into other galaxies awaits. It's all in the green.

Patience and a steady gaze, he said and took my hand. We
stood on his deck. Leaned into the railing. Looked out
at the ocean. Waves slowly in and away. How fast is a second?

It could be a blink, a sigh, a gasp.

Or the leaves of the ash tree skittering suddenly.

I look out the Upstairs Window
after Steve Kowit

Once in a while, after a rainy few days, I look
out into the consequence of the evening and know dying:
a family member and dear friend calls. Remember Paul?
He sprinted everywhere, guzzled his food, smiled
at strangers. He actually escorted ladies across
busy streets. Always laughing. His wife said he passed
in his sleep, a heart attack. *Merciful God*, I whisper
to an empty room. So soon? I recall his face, his smile.
Another evening, when the palm trees are dripping,
I open the window. Inhale. My friend Ryan, his voice
so low I don't recognize him, says George succumbed.
I think: *he was valedictorian and a generous soul.*
I wish him eternal peace. The serenity of the evening pauses.
Yet there is no easing back into sleep. Where did all those years
go? The passage of time hovers below the realm of love.
Memories, freed now from over-thinking, emerge.
Swim into consciousness. Some clear as a sunny day.
Like Winston, brown and thin in wet baggy trunks, going to buy beer
at the corner store, me calling out the window: don't
forget the cigarettes! Grinning as he comes out; Budweiser,
Marlboros, and two cokes for later, just to enjoy the buzz
of being together. The car radio playing Jim Croce, puff clouds
moving in on an early summer evening.

Stay Clear of the Doors

1.I heard him stumbling up the steps, footfall heavy. 2. He bumped into the sides of the hallway. Giggled. 3. I knew to go to another room and act as if nothing is awry. 4. His entry tells it all: level of intoxication, mood, and most importantly how much time before the pass-out, which could be on the couch, in the bedroom or on any floor. 5. I see, when it is all over and quiet resumes, the green of the leaves. I leave to take a walk through the sludge of my disquiet.

OLIVE MOON

lemon
How strange to see the glass arrive with a sugar rind
on the rim; this one is called a lemon drop curling
but across the bar sits a man with one over
that has two green olives, slayed the
with a decorated pick, frills edge
of red, shooting boldly
from the top, as if
to say: drink
prudently
so
no
so
no
so
no
so
no
so
no
one sees
the longing
lingering touch
of my fingers reaching,
on the glass and the olive moon the olive moon
stretching over the river.

Japanese Gardens Revisited

Everyone has someone who loves them. Forever, like
a brother or a best friend. A lover. I knew I loved him

as I will love none other in my life, yet not in a kissing,
hand-holding, under the sheets on a hot summer

evening way. He taught me how to stay with the sky,
to find Sagittarius. We laughed and climbed the maples

at night. High in the branches we sat. Watched evening strollers
underneath. Suspended above, in the dark he quoted Ezra Pound:

*I stood still and was a tree among the wood/knowing the truth
of things unseen before.* He scoffed at astrologers, except Ansara

who told us that our love was palpable. He gave me the book
Japanese Gardens Revisited, mailed from his base in Okinawa.

He is so far away now. Marriages away. A divorce away.
Climates away. I insisted on naming my first child Patrick.

I was reckless in college; impulsive, charming, smart
and distant. Patrick laughed, reciting Ezra Pound:

And the days are not full enough, and the nights are not full enough.
We fell asleep side by side after imagining the Moss Garden

at Heisen-ji. I am quieter now. Guarded. I leave
gatherings early. Read. Inspect the seven varieties of foliage

surrounding the gardens. Marvel at different bonsais, their
placement.
And life slips by like a field mouse, not shaking the grass.

Rest with Me

Rest with me,
my melancholy.
I find quiet
with difficulty.
Better to move.
I recognize the sinking,
spiraling sensation
in my moldy chest.
Something, like a small marble
is stuck. Heavy. I notice
my breath
in and out of my throat
filling then emptying my
lungs. Lungs like rain boots.
I swallow over
the floating pebbles
of goodbyes.

Squirrel Neighborhoods

A cold morning and we are nestled
in bed, a white down comforter
up to our necks. I rise. Walk
to the warmer kitchen.
Make coffee. Into the starling
morning I see one in the gnarled
top of the apple tree.
In nearby maples four more
nests appear. Squirrels
live in neighborhoods too.
Scamper. Play. Scrounge.
Outsmart birdfeeder
owners. Hoard acorns.
We all hold on to something,
like medals from races.
Or feelings of isolation,
even when snuggled together.
Squirrels nose the ground
with cardinals, pigeons.
Gather nuts, like thoughts,
to carry home. I think
of winter sledding. Of being so cold
I forget my fading fondness.
We share this apple tree. The yard.
The squirrels remind me
of my running. Three miles today.
Of my collecting apples alone in the fall
for cider. For making pies.
Once in for the evening, we
settle into the quiet while
the pine voles navigate
their night tunnels. While
owls call, asking to be heard.

Kimono

She wears the blue kimono with soft pink
apple blossoms every Sunday.
The sleeves, when she raises her arms, reveal
an entire tree, bees gracing rosy blossom
centers. Sometimes, in bare feet, she goes outside,
into the car, and drives through the town
with the windows open, wind blowing,
V-shaped sleeves covering the cup holder.
She can't forget the late-night jeep rides in South Korea.
Bumping with no seat belts to the Front. And back with the dying.
The hospital built outside the action.
She knew. Some saw oiled and perfumed
arms comforting in those sleeves, others, whore.
Her life now is in Maine, in her small house,
away from her two sons who never call.
The Colonel visits every Sunday,
sleeps over, makes waffles, leaves.
Without her, he knows he would wither,
have to reckon his life to a chapter,
like a *life phase*, such as the appointed
therapist calls re-entry.

Free Advice

Listen to the news,
unraveling the depression
of the last shooter,
chronicling his younger years
and then wonder about your
childhood, with drinking
and forgetful parents, like when
you rode on the back
of Tracy's motorcycle,
wind cold on your face.
They just let you go. Waved
to both of you.
Many decades
later now and you search
for that joyful impulse,
that knowing, as quickly
as when you drank shots
merrily, in Wisconsin.
When you were hired
to teach for the first time,
you kept planning, kept
reading. Your constant curiosity
fell into the Spring mudslide, but
you knew. You told yourself:
Listen to the moments. Rassle
apart your fears. One BIG one must
have lived in the shooter's brain.
Make a promise to yourself
to notice, to help, to laugh,
to pray, and wrapped up
in all of this take the free advice
living in your soul.

The Girl Who Sulks

She slithers into her seat,
late, takes out her book,
lays her hand atop her pencil case.
Slouches, like a housecat
almost ready to finish bathing.
She wears her hair long,
meticulously combed.
She never tosses her head.
She never smiles.
She never offers answers.
Yet, like her dark hair, streaked
with auburn, she is diligently
prepared. Insightful. Daring,
in her written analyses.
Today we study Neruda's
"If You Forget Me".
One student offers: *Neruda*
writes of conditional love,
using 'if…then'. Some agree.
Another adds: *he, Neruda,*
is crazy-in-love. He wants
to know if she is in his world.
Our eyes lock. I ask her opinion,
suffering the glare. I wait,
nearly ready to break
the uncomfortable silence
by moving the class into groups.

She straightens. Takes a mechanical
pencil in her hand, holding
her talisman. Says: *Neruda's love*
definition is like a flowing past tense.
You can't forget how a log feels,
if you sit on it, for instance,
or a fire, like at camp,
or the red maple leaves, or

how someone made you feel.
No matter his macho bravado
about "forgetting" gesturing air quotes.
Silence. She sits up.
All eyes turn as she runs her fingers
through her hair.

Again

Tired at the end of the day,
with dinner preparations looming,
homework to check,
fighting to referee, I wish
I had it all to do over again.
That I was not so vacant. My energy
flowed into my job. Oh, to have
more joy with my own children:
playing more, laughing more,
together, just together.

Sunlight Breaks the Waves

sunlight breaks the waves
sandpipers skitter the world
you, love, the center.

Pebbles

pebbles in unmoving
puddles clouds color water white
starlings screen the heavens.

Sharing Cake

In my memory Roberto and Darcy
chanted their way into the bakery
on Fifth Avenue, all blissed out
after yoga, starving for sugar.
Let's split the chocolate cake,
Darcy said, so *fucking good here.*

Roberto's fingers, with the fudge
icing clinging, pointed to a lemon bar.
This too! he sang. Everyone looked
up from coffee, from oatmeal,
from newspapers, and were so fucking
drawn into the present moment.

Life on the Edge

I sense the necessity of life
in the woods. I need constant
reminders of the leaves in me
shimmering in the afternoon light.
More tangible than deadlines or visits
where I forget the smell of the applewood
or the birch or the waves that sprawl
and kiss the shore nearby. I am never quite
sure of anything unless I walk on discarded
needles. Unless I touch a trunk. Find a crow's
feather. Know the great weight of life outside of me.
I return to cook dinner for a hungry husband,
feed the Labrador. I dither remembering
the pines; select orange linen napkins
to nourish the stained and sanguine narrow
beach of my heart.

Nancy spends summer and fall in New Hampshire and Pennsylvania and now winters in Naples, Florida. This recent snowbird move to Florida offers explorations of tropical habitats. She is drawn to water in its many iterations: lakes, the sea, canals, rivers, rain, and puddles! She spent her childhood years in Santiago, Chile and Evreux, France, in the Normandy province, as a daughter in an Air Force family. She used to play soccer for a team named "Las Amas de Casa". She volunteers for Habitat for Humanity and is a docent at the Art Institute in Naples, FL. She holds an undergraduate degree from the University of WI, Madison and an MA from the University of New Hampshire, Durham. She is the founder of Wheaton Writing Academy.